WELCOME

Welcome to our World Fusion Plant Based Soul Food Recipe Book. We trust that our gourmet recipes will tantalize your taste buds, support good health, as well as a more sustainable way of eating on the planet. Our cuisine is simple to make, delicious and inspiring. For equipment, we mainly use a large cast iron skillet, a food processor, a Vitamix and an immersion hand blender. We cook with lots of love, whole foods, spices and fresh organic produce, as locally sourced as possible. We believe as stated by Hippocrates "let food be thy medicine, and medicine be thy food" and our intention with this cookbook is to inspire others to create delicious, healthy, yummy, vegetarian, diverse meals. We hope that this cookbook will inspire people towards a more plant based way of eating that supports optimal health, wellness and the planet! Scientists say that a planetary health diet (which allows for 1 beef burger and 2 servings of fish per week) would prevent millions of deaths per year and turn the course of climate change. So happy plant based cooking!

Warmly,
Heather & Donny

TABLE OF CONTENTS

INTRODUCTION	l.
**SIDES	CHAPTER 1**	01
Roasted Acorn Arugula Salad	02
Cesar Salad	03
Sweet Salsa	04
Guacamole	04
Hummus	05
Carrot Tahini Salad	06
Olive Tapenade	06
Salad Dressings	07
Chickpea Croutons	08
Cashew or Mac Nut Cream	08
Mac Nut Cheese	09
Crispy Shallots Salad Topper	09
Mexican Corn Salsa	10
Bean Salad	11
Pan Roasted Rosemary Potatoes	12
Turmeric Herbed Quinoa	13
Tex Mex Sweet Potato Fritters	14
Indian Spinach	15
Curried Cauliflower	15
Green Papaya Salad	16
Savory Brussel Sprouts	17
**SOUPS	CHAPTER 2**	18
Black Bean Soup	19
Potato, Leak, & Cauliflower Soup	20
Portobello Mushroom Soup	21
Vegetable Chili	22
Butternut Squash Soup	23
Pho Noodle Soup	24
Red Lentil & Chickpea Soup	25
Coconut & Lentil Vegetable Soup	26

TABLE OF CONTENTS

**ENTREES	CHAPTER 3**	27
<u>Mushroom Lentil Grain Bowl</u>	28
Pasta with Balsamic Reduction	29
Curried Kale & Butternut Squash	30
Vegan Walnut Pesto Penne	31
Stuffed Portobello Mushrooms	32
Mashed Sweet Potatos	33
Caramelized Onions	33
Portobella Mushroom Tacos	33
Teriyaki Stir Fry	34
Spaghetti Squash Primavera	35
Dahl	36
Jahawaiian Tempeh Wraps	37
Tempeh TLT Sandwich	38
Chana Masala	39
**SWEETS	CHAPTER 4**	40
Cinnamon Apple Crisp	41
Banana Bread	42
Sacred Cacao Bites	43
About Sacred Cacao	44
Giving Thanks	45
Thank You Credits	46
Notes & Reflections	47

SIDES

CHAPTER 1

ROASTED ACORN ARUGULA SALAD & TAHINI DRESSING
SERVES 4 | FEATURED ON CHAPTER COVER PAGE

TAHINI DRESSING
½ cup tahini
¼ cup lemon juice
3 tbl fresh parsley or cilantro, chopped
3 cloves garlic, minced
1-2 tbl maple syrup
¼ cup water

BALSAMIC REDUCTION SAUCE
1 cup Balsamic Vinegar
Place in a small saucepan and simmer for 12 minutes until it reduces by approximately 1/2 the volume. Be sure not to let it boil over as it can burn. Then turn off and remove from heat.

ROASTED ACORN SQUASH
1 medium acorn squash, sliced small chunks
¼ cup olive oil

Clean the skin of the squash. Then cut in half and remove seeds and set them aside. Next, cut the squash into ½" think small chunks. Coat with olive oil and roast at 350 for 30 minutes until cooked.

TOASTED SQUASH SEEDS
Clean and dry the seeds. Either air fry for 10 minutes or bake in the oven for 30 minutes until crispy.

HOW TO MAKE DRESSING
Add everything except the water to a bowl and whisk together. Add water a little at a time until it reaches the desired consistency. Can be refrigerated for up to 5 days.

HOW TO MAKE SALAD
Place a large package of Arugula, cleaned into a salad bowl. Dress with Tahini dressing, mix up until consistency of a caesar salad. Then add in the roasted acorn squash. Sprinkle in ½ cup of mix of roasted pumpkin seeds and dried fruits such as cranberries. Finally with a spoon, dollop the macadamia nut cheese (p. 9) on top and drizzle balsamic reduction sauce over the salad.

CAESAR SALAD
PREP 1 HR | SERVES 4-6

DRESSING
½ cup raw cashews, tahini or mac nuts
1 garlic clove
2 tsp fresh lemon juice
2 tsp Dijon mustard

2 tsp capers, drained
2 tbl Nutritional Yeast
½ cup water
Freshly ground black pepper

HOW TO MAKE
First debone and then chop 1 large bundle of kale leaves. Lightly coat and rub with 1 tbl olive oil and a pinch of salt and massage the kale for about 3 to 4 minutes until tender. Then coat the kale with the dressing and toss. Lastly, top with roasted chickpeas (p. 8) and serve!

SWEET SALSA

PREP 10 MIN | SERVES 6

INGREDIENTS
2 cups tomatoes, diced
1 scallion, chopped
2 sprigs cilantro or parsley, chopped
¼ cup lemon juice
½ cup olive oil
1 pinch salt
½ mango chopped (optional)
½ jalepeño, thinly sliced (optional)

HOW TO MAKE
Mix tomatoes, scallion, cilantro, mango, and jalepeño in one bowl. Set aside. In a separate bowl, whisk lemon juice, olive oil, and salt until evenly mixed. Combine with first bowl and serve.

GUACAMOLE

PREP 10 MIN | SERVES 6

INGREDIENTS
3 avocados, diced
1 scallion, minced
2 sprigs fresh cilantro or parsley, chopped
1 cup tomatoes, diced
1 tsp salt
4-6 tbl lemon juice

HOW TO MAKE
Use fork to mix all ingredients together. Mash until texture is evenly mixed, leaving chunky.

HUMMUS
PREP 12 MIN | SERVES 6

BASE INGREDIENTS
3 cups of cooked garbanzo beans
½ cup of olive oil
5 cloves of garlic
1 tsp of himalayan salt
2 heaping tbl of tahini
½ cup of water
2 tbl of lemon juice
sprig of parsley
paprika powder (optional)

OPTIONAL ADDITIONS
Add roasted red peppers, olives, sun dried tomatoes, cilantro, parsley, lime, lemon.

Pairs well with crackers, veggies and can be used as a sauce for a wrap.

HOW TO MAKE
Blend in food processor or strongest blender available until smooth. Garnish with parsley and paprika powder (optional).

CARROT TAHINI SALAD
PREP 10 MIN | SERVES 4

INGREDIENTS
½ cup tahini
3 cups baby carrots or large carrots
¼ cup lemon juice
1 tsp salt

HOW TO MAKE
Use food processor or hand grater to grate carrots. Place grated carrots in bowl and add tahini, lemon juice and salt and stir until incorporated.
Serve as a side dish, topping, or as a dipping sauce!

OLIVE TAPENADE
PREP 10 MIN | SERVES 4

HOW TO MAKE
Blend in food processor until smooth. Stir in capers.

INGREDIENTS
4 cups of kalamata olives
1 shallot, roughly chopped
1 cup olive oil
¼ cup parsley, chopped
4 tbl apple cider vinegar
¼ cup capers

SALAD DRESSINGS

HOT CHILI PEPPER SAUCE
2 cups Hawaiian chili peppers
3 cups apple cider vinegar

Place ingredients into a food processor or blender and pulse until the chili peppers are chopped up. Place in jar. Store in fridge! If it's too spicy, add more vinegar.

TURMERIC DRESSING
1 cup freshly ground turmeric
1 cup olive oil
1 cup lemon juice
3 heaping tsp black pepper

Incorporate all together and whisk. Serve atop a fresh green salad.

BALSAMIC DRESSING
¼ cup olive oil
¼ cup balsamic
2 tbl maple syrup

Whisk all together.

LILIKOI DRESSING
¼ cup olive oil
¼ cup lemon juice
1 cup lilikoi

Whisk all together. If too tart add 2 tbl maple syrup.

CHICKPEA CROUTONS
PREP 15 MIN | SERVES 4

INGREDIENTS
2 cups cooked chickpeas
3 tbl olive oil
3 tbl garlic and parsley powder
1 tsp salt

HOW TO MAKE
Heat oil in skillet. Sauté chickpeas until golden brown and crispy. When done, turn off heat and toss in garlic and parsley powder and salt to taste. Delicious in soup, as a salad topping or in a rice pilaf!

CASHEW OR MAC NUT CREAM
PREP 15 MIN | SERVES 4

INGREDIENTS
2 cups raw cashews or Macadamia Nuts
(soaked in water for 4 hours)
2 cups water
½ tsp lemon juice
½ tsp nutritional yeast
Pinch salt

HOW TO MAKE
Put all ingredients in blender and blend until smooth. Add more water if you want it more saucy. Also makes for a nice salad dressing.

MAC NUT CHEESE

INGREDIENTS
1.5 cups macadamia nuts, soaked 4 hours
2 tbl lemon juice
2 tbl nutritional yeast
1 garlic clove, minced
¼ tsp Himalayan salt
¼ - ½ cup water
¼ cup cilantro or parsley

HOW TO MAKE
In a food processor place macadamia nuts, lemon juice, nutritional yeast, garlic, salt and ¼ cup water. Pulse until the consistency of crumbled ricotta cheese. If more water is needed, add a little at a time. When desired consistency is reached, pulse in cilantro or parsley. Do not over blend.

CRISPY SHALLOTS

INGREDIENTS
4 large shallots, sliced
1 cup gluten free flour
4 tbl, coconut oil

HOW TO MAKE
Break up the shallot slices into rings (think onion rings). Then toss in the flour and cover thoroughly. Heat coconut oil on medium high in a skillet/cast iron pan. When hot, pan fry the shallots until crispy.

MEXICAN CORN SALSA
PREP 30 MIN | SERVES 4-6

INGREDIENTS

4 cups of fresh or frozen corn
2 cups macadamia nuts, soaked for 8 hours
3 cups water
1 tbl Nutritional Yeast
1 tbl chilli powder

2 medium lemons, juiced
1 medium sized pickle, diced
3 baby bell peppers, diced
2 cups pineapple, diced
¼ cup cilantro, roughly chopped

HOW TO MAKE

Lightly char corn cornels in a dry cast iron pan. Then transfer to the fridge or freezer to chill for about 30 minutes. Rinse soaked macadamia nuts and place in blender along with water, nutritional yeast, and chili powder. Blend until smooth, then add the lime juice and blend gently until incorporated. Then pour the sauce over the corn and add in the rest of the ingredients and stir.

BEAN SALAD

PREP 15 MIN | SERVES 6

INGREDIENTS
¼ cup chives or red onion, diced
2 sprigs fresh parsley, chopped
1 cup red wine vinegar
1 tsp maple syrup
½ cup olive oil
½ tsp garlic powder
½ tsp salt
½ tsp black pepper
1 cup corn niblets
2 sweet baby peppers, diced
2 cups strained and rinsed beans, kidney or black or both.

HOW TO MAKE
Whisk together onion, red wine vinegar, maple syrup, olive oil, garlic powder, salt, and black pepper. Set aside as dressing.

Combine beans, corn, and sweet baby peppers in a bowl and incorporate dressing. Serve cold.

PAN ROASTED ROSEMARY POTATOES
PREP 25 MIN | SERVES 4

INGREDIENTS
4 cups baby potatoes (quartered or halved)
½ cup coconut oil
2 tbl olive oil
2 tbl garlic powder
2 tbl parsley
2 tbl fresh or dried rosemary and thyme
1 tsp himalayan salt

HOW TO MAKE
Prepare potatoes by cutting into quarters or halves, then rinse with water. Heat coconut and olive oil in a cast iron pan. When hot, add potatoes and pan fry, turning over frequently until golden brown. When done, turn off heat, toss in garlic powder, salt and herbs.

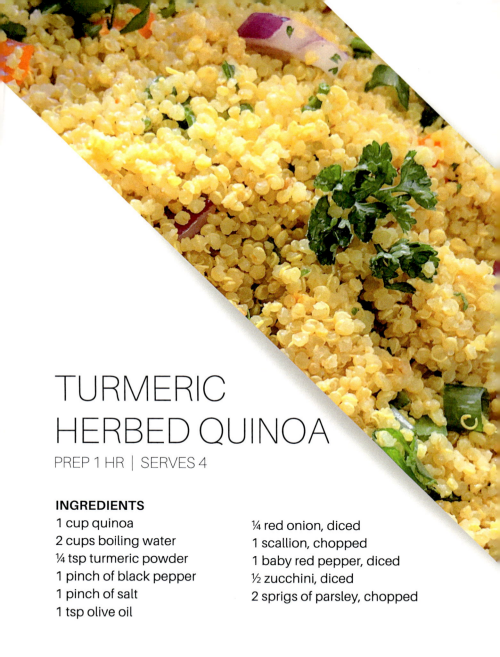

TURMERIC HERBED QUINOA

PREP 1 HR | SERVES 4

INGREDIENTS

1 cup quinoa
2 cups boiling water
¼ tsp turmeric powder
1 pinch of black pepper
1 pinch of salt
1 tsp olive oil

¼ red onion, diced
1 scallion, chopped
1 baby red pepper, diced
½ zucchini, diced
2 sprigs of parsley, chopped

HOW TO MAKE

Cook quinoa in pot or rice cooker along with turmeric, black pepper, pinch of salt and olive oil. When cooked, add in veggies at the end and mix up!

TEX MEX VEGGIE FRITTERS
PREP 1 HR | SERVES 4-6

INGREDIENTS
8 cups potatoes
2 large carrots
1 medium zucchini
1 small red or sweet white onion, thinly sliced
4 tbl Bob's Red Mill All Purpose Gluten Free Flour
4 tbl Mexican seasoning or chili powder
¼ cup coconut oil

HOW TO MAKE
Grate potatoes, carrots and zucchini in food processor. Thinly slice onion. Mix everything together in large mixing bowl. Add spices to the mixture. Heat a few tablespoons of oil in pan and make thin patties. Cook for approximately 5 minutes on each side.

Serve with cashew cream (p. 8), Mexican corn salsa (p. 10)! Delicious!

INDIAN SPINACH
PREP 15 MIN | SERVES 4

INGREDIENTS
8 cups raw spinach
4 tbl olive oil
1 pinch of salt
1 tbl garlic powder
1 tsp chili powder

HOW TO MAKE
Pour about 4 tablespoons of olive oil into a cast iron pan, at medium heat warm oil and add in the spinach. Sauté the spinach until all the water has evaporated. Then incorporate garlic powder, chili powder and salt to taste.

CURRIED CAULIFLOWER
PREP 15 MIN | SERVES 4

INGREDIENTS
½ cauliflower head, cut into florets
¼ cup olive oil
2 tsp curry powder
1 pinch of salt

HOW TO MAKE
Heat ¼ cup olive oil in cast iron pan. When hot, add cauliflower. Pan fry the cauliflower until golden brown (about 7 minutes).

When crisp and tender, turn off heat and sprinkle with curry powder and salt to taste. Toss to incorporate.

GREEN PAPAYA SALAD
PREP 15 MIN | Serves 4

INGREDIENTS
3 cups green papaya, grated or julienned
1 carrot, grated or julienned
½ cup chives, chopped
or red or sweet onions, slivered
½ cup raw cashews, whole (optional)
⅓ cup rice or plum vinegar
3 tbl maple syrup
3 tbl tamari
1 small chili pepper, minced
¼ cup mint and/or cilantro,
roughly chopped

HOW TO MAKE
Prepare papaya, carrot and chives. Use food processor to grate if available. Mix together vinegar, maple syrup, and tamari and chili pepper. Pour liquid over vegetables and toss lightly. Top with cashews, cilantro and mint.

SAVORY BRUSSELS SPROUTS
PREP 15 MIN | SERVES 4

INGREDIENTS
4 cups brussels sprouts, halved
¼ sweet onion, diced
3 tbl olive oil
splash of balsamic vinegar

HOW TO MAKE
Heat olive oil in cast iron pan. When hot, add in brussels sprouts and pan fry until crispy. Then add in onions and sauté until soft. When everything is done, splash with balsamic vinegar generously, lightly sauté and turn heat off. Add a pinch of salt and serve.

Lovely with cashew or macadamia nut cream (p. 8)

SOUPS

CHAPTER 2

BLACK BEAN SOUP
PREP 40 MIN | SERVES 4

INGREDIENTS
4 cups black beans cooked
4 cups vegetable broth
1 tbl olive oil
1 large onion, chopped
1 stalk celery, chopped
4 cloves garlic, minced
2 tbl chili powder
1 tbl ground cumin
1 pinch black pepper
2 cups crushed tomatoes
2 cups organic corn kernels (optional)

HOW TO MAKE
Heat oil in large pot and sauté onions, celery, carrots and garlic for 5 minutes. Add in chili powder, cumin and black pepper and stir, incorporating for 1 minute. Add in vegetable broth, 1 cup of beans and bring to a boil.

Separately, in a blender or food processor add 3 cups of beans and tomatoes and blend until smooth.
Stir into soup mixture and reduce heat to medium and simmer for 15 minutes.

A optional addition to this soup is to add in about 2 cups of organic corn kernels. Add to the last 5 minutes of final cooking.

Nice to top with a dollop of Mac Nut or Cashew Cream (p. 8) and chopped cilantro, as well as guacamole (p. 4) and chips!

POTATO, LEEK, & CAULIFLOWER SOUP
PREP 45 MIN | SERVES 6

INGREDIENTS
4 large potatoes cut in 1 inch quarters
1 whole onion, diced
2 cups celery, diced
4 tbl thyme, dried or fresh
1 vegetable bouillon
2 tbl olive oil
1 tsp salt
6 cups water
4 cups cauliflower, roughly chopped
2 leeks, chopped
6 cloves garlic, minced

HOW TO MAKE
Add potatoes, onion, celery, thyme, vegetable bouillon, olive oil, salt, and water into rice cooker. Push soup button and let be as soup base cooks. Sauté olive oil, cauliflower, leeks, and garlic. Then purée until smooth.

Mix soup base and purée and serve hot on a cold day!

PORTOBELLO MUSHROOM SOUP
PREP 40 | SERVES 4

INGREDIENTS
7 portobello mushrooms
¼ cup of olive oil
1 sweet white onion
4 cloves of garlic (roughly chopped)
2 cubes of vegetable bouillon (non msg)
8 sprigs of fresh thyme
1 pinch salt
1 pinch pepper
1 can or 2 cups of coconut milk

HOW TO MAKE
Scoop out the inner brown gills of the mushrooms and discard. Dice mushrooms. Dice onion. Heat up olive oil in a skillet. Sauté mushrooms and onions together. Add garlic to the vegetables. Boil 4 cups of water. Add 2 cubes of vegetable bouillon to boiling water. Add sautéed vegetables to the broth. Add 8 sprigs of fresh thyme to the broth. Add a tsp of salt and a tsp of pepper. Blend the broth with wand or blender. Add 1 can or 2 cups of coconut milk to broth and blend.

VEGETABLE CHILI
PREP 45 MIN | SERVES 4

INGREDIENTS
1 medium sweet onion, diced
3 cloves garlic, minced
2 tbl olive oil
3 tbl chili powder
3 tbl raw honey or maple syrup
2 cups/16 oz of strained tomatoes
2 cups water
1 medium sweet potato cut in 1" cubes
6 crimini or baby portobello mushrooms, quartered
½ cup corn niblets
½ cup peas
½ cup cauliflower
½ tsp salt
½ tsp black pepper

HOW TO MAKE
Heat oil in pot. Then cook onions and garlic until tender and brown. Stir in chili powder and sauté for 1 minute until fragrant. Add the strained tomatoes, water, salt and pepper. Bring to a boil and add the sweet potatoes. Turn down to simmer and cook for 10 minutes until the sweet potatoes are tender. Prick with fork to check. Finally add in the sweetener and the rest of the vegetables. Cook for another 5 to 10 minutes until everything is incorporated and warm. Delicious served over rice.

BUTTERNUT SQUASH SOUP
PREP 40 MIN | SERVES 4

INGREDIENTS
1 medium butternut squash, skinned and cut into 2" cubes
1 small container organic coconut milk
2 inch piece of ginger, minced
2 tbl garlic, minced
1 cup leeks or onion, chopped
4 tbl thyme (fresh or dried)
1 tsp himalayan salt
1 tsp black pepper

HOW TO MAKE
Heat 1 tbl coconut oil in pot on medium-high heat. Sauté onions and garlic until tender. Add water, squash and thyme and bring to a boil. Then turn down heat to medium until squash is tender, about 20 minutes. Place everything blender or use a immersion hand blender and add the coconut milk, ginger, salt and pepper and blend until smooth. Return to pot and season to taste with more salt or pepper as necessary. Top with chickpea croutons (p. 8), brussels sprouts (p. 17), as well as, cashew cream (p. 8), and fresh cilantro!

PHO NOODLE SOUP

PREP 45 MIN | SERVES 4

INGREDIENTS
2 Veggie Boullion Cubes (No MSG)
8 cups of water
1 thumb of ginger, thinly sliced
1 whole star anise pod
1 cup mushrooms, sliced
½ cup sweet potatoes, small cubes
½ cup carrots, thinly sliced
6 small/medium boc choy, whole
½ sweet onion sliced, slivered

TOPPINGS (don't cook)
1 scallion, chopped
½ cup mung beans
2 sprigs of basil and mint
2 sprigs of parsley, chopped
1 cup mac nuts or peanuts, roughly chopped

For Vietnamese rice noodles, follow the recipe on the package.

HOW TO MAKE
Boil 8 cups of water, add sliced bouillon cubes, star anise and ginger. Simmer for 15 minutes. In separate pan, heat coconut oil on medium high heat and sauté all veggies except boc choy for 5 minutes. Then remove vegetables from pan. Next steam boc choy with ½ cup water in pan for 2 minutes. Cook the Vietnamese Rice Noodles and drain. Place noodles in bowls, top with vegetables and scoop broth over. Add toppings and serve! Also excellent topped with our special sweet tamari green papaya dressing.

RED LENTIL & CHICKPEA SOUP
PREP 45 MIN | SERVES 4

INGREDIENTS
2½ cups red lentils
1½ cups cooked chickpeas
8 cups vegetable stock
1 small onion, diced
3 cloves garlic, minced
1 tbl tomato paste
1 bay leaf
1½ tsp cumin
2 tbl olive oil
salt and pepper to taste

HOW TO MAKE
Heat oil in pot and sauté garlic and onions until soft, about 5 minutes. Add vegetable stock, tomato paste, bay leaf, cumin and lentils. Bring to a boil and then turn down to medium low heat for about 20 minutes until lentils are done. Add salt and pepper to taste and serve.

COCONUT & LENTIL VEGETABLE SOUP
PREP 40 MIN | SERVES 4

INGREDIENTS
3 cups broccoli florets
2 cups of butternut squash, cut into 1" cubes
3 cloves garlic, minced
1 small sweet onion, diced
½ tsp ground coriander
½ tsp ground cumin
2 tbl ginger, minced
1 tsp turmeric, minced or powdered
6 cups water
3 vegetable boullion cubes (no msg)
½ cup brown lentils
1 can coconut milk
1 tbl coconut oil

HOW TO MAKE
Heat coconut oil in pot and cook onions and garlic until soft. Add spices and stir for a minute until fragrances release. Add water and bring to boil and then add the lentils. Cook lentils for about 30 minutes then add the butternut squash and continue cooking for another 10 minutes until both are done. Finally, when cooked, add in broccoli and whatever other vegetables you like (corn, mushrooms, etc.). Then turn heat down to low and stir in the coconut milk. Once incorporated, turn heat off. Do not allow the coconut milk to curdle. Serve. Great topped with hot sauce!

ENTRÉES

CHAPTER 3

MUSHROOM LENTIL GRAIN BOWL & MISO DRESSING
SERVES 4 | FEATURED ON CHAPTER COVERPAGE

BOWL INGREDIENTS
1 ½ cooked brown Lentils - ½ cup dry lentils and 1 ½ cups water, plus one vegetable bouillon, simmer covered for about 20 minutes.

3 cups quinoa - 1 cup dry quinoa and 1 ½ cups water, simmer covered about 15 minutes or use a rice cooker. Tip - make extra crispy by pan frying in coconut oil once cooked.

6 cups of assorted mushrooms sliced (ali'i, shitake, and oyster), sliced - in a large skillet saute cook over medium heat for 10 minutes and then splash with 2 to 3 tbl tamari

9 cups fresh clean spinach

¼ red onion, thinly sliced

3 cups of radicchio lettuce, shredded

3 baby bell pepper julienned

1 cup dried cranberries

MISO DRESSING
⅓ cup seasoned rice vinegar
2 tbl tahini
1 tbl maple syrup
1 tbl yellow or white miso
1 tbl tamari (gluten free)
1 tsp garlic powder
1 tsp Toasted sesame oil
2 - 3 tbl Water
¼-½" piece ginger, minced (optional)
Dash of black pepper, if desired

HOW TO MAKE DRESSING
Add all of the ingredients to a medium bowl and whisk until smooth. Will store in an airtight container in the fridge for up to 7 days.

PUT BOWL TOGETHER
Place spinach in a large mixing bowl and mix in red onions, radicchio lettuce, and baby bell peppers. Then transfer to 4 serving bowls. Top with quinoa, lentils, mushrooms, dried cranberries and miso dressing.

PASTA WITH BALSAMIC REDUCTION
PREP 40 MIN | SERVES 4

INGREDIENTS
1 medium red onion, slivered
3 cloves garlic, minced
2 tbl olive oil
¼ cup balsamic vinegar
¼ cup water
1 package caserecce or spiral or bow tie noodles
8 crimini or baby portobello mushrooms, sliced
½ cup cherry tomatoes
½ cup kalamata olives
4 cups baby spinach
½ tsp salt
pepper to taste

HOW TO MAKE
Cook noodles and set aside. Heat oil in cast iron pan and caramelize onions and then add garlic. Cook for another minute and douse with balsamic vinegar. Add mushrooms and sauté for another coupe of minutes. Toss in tomatoes for 2 minutes. Then add noodles and incorporate. Add water and a little more balsamic vinegar if necessary to have a nice coating. Add salt to taste. Finally incorporate spinach and turn heat off. The spinach will wilt with the heat of the pasta. Top with olives and serve.

CURRIED KALE & BUTTERNUT SQUASH
PREP 40 MIN | SERVES 4

INGREDIENTS

1 cup rice, or quinoa, or both
½ butternut squash, cubed
½ sweet onion, diced
2-3 cloves garlic, minced
1 ginger finger, 3-4 inches long, minced finely
3 tbl olive oil
1 bunch kale, rinsed and chopped
1-2 tbl honey
½ cup coconut cream
½ tsp salt
½ tsp black pepper
½ tsp cumin

HOW TO MAKE

Tip for cubing: First cut or peel off skin. Then chop in halves, quarters, slices, and cubes, getting smaller with each cut!

Cube butternut squash and steam by pouring hot water over squash. Cover for 10 minutes and set aside.

Heat skillet with olive oil. Add onions and garlic and sauté until soft. Add cumin.

Add 3 cups of water, add fresh ginger, coconut cream, and honey. Simmer 3 minutes.

Fold in kale. Cover and reduce to low until kale is wilted for 2 minutes. Serve with steamed rice or quinoa or both.

VEGAN WALNUT PESTO

PREP TIME: 15 MIN

INGREDIENTS
4 cups basil leaves
1 cup walnuts (soaked in water for 4 hours then drained)
¼ cup raw garlic, coarsely chopped
1 cup olive oil
⅓ cup lemon juice
1 tsp salt

HOW TO MAKE
Place everything in a food processor and puree until a consistency you like.

MORE PESTO IDEAS

- Pesto is also great over steamed vegetables such as asparagus and green beans.
- Serve pesto as a dip with crackers or veggies.
- Use pesto as a spread over toast or bread.
- Pesto can also be made with other leafy greens like kale, spinach or gotu kola.

PENNE WITH PESTO

PREP TIME: 30 MIN | SERVES 4

INGREDIENTS
1 package of penne pasta, cooked
5 baby portobello mushrooms, thinly sliced
1 cup cherry tomatoes
4 garlic cloves, minced
¼ cup olive oil

HOW TO MAKE
Heat olive oil in cast iron pan. Sauté mushrooms (put lid on to create juices for a couple of minutes). Then add chopped garlic and sauté until brown.

Then turn off heat and add penne pasta in and pour about 2 cups of pesto on top and incorporate by stirring.

Then add in cherry tomatoes and sauté for another minute.

STUFFED PORTOBELLO MUSHROOMS

PREP 45 MIN | SERVES 4

INGREDIENTS
4 portobello mushrooms (gilled & cleaned)
1 cup rice and quinoa, mixed, cooked
1 small sweet potato, cubed
½ sweet onion, diced
2 cloves garlic, chopped fine
1 block tempeh, cubed (optional)

SEASONING
ASIAN STYLE
splash of tamari
-or-
SAVORY STYLE
dash of pepper,
oregano, & thyme

HOW TO MAKE
Sauté onions and sweet potatoes in olive oil. Add garlic in when nearly done. Sauté tempeh until crispy. Add everything to rice mixture and then add seasonings. For asian style add a splash of tamari. For savory flavors add a dash of pepper, thyme and oregano. Then cook mushrooms in pan until tender. Don't over cook. Just a couple of minutes on each side. Cover with lid for a minute to get juices going. Then stuff the mushrooms with the rice mixture.

NOTE: You can use this same recipe and stuff blanched large peppers.

MASHED SWEET POTATOES
PREP 15 MIN

INGREDIENTS
1 large sweet potato chopped
1 tbl coconut oil

Boil Sweet Potato for about 15 minutes until soft. Then drain off water. Finally, add in coconut oil and mash until smooth.

CARMELIZED ONIONS
PREP 10 MIN

INGREDIENTS
1 large sweet onion
4 tbl olive oil
1 tsp balsamic vinegar

Slice onion in half and then into ¼ inch slices (rings)
Sauté onion in olive oil until soft. Then douse with balsamic vinegar.

PORTOBELLA MUSHROOM TACOS
PREP 15 MIN | SERVES 4

INGREDIENTS
4 large or 12 small portobello mushrooms (gilled + sliced into ¼" slices)
2 garlic cloves minced
1 tbl Mexican or chili seasoning
4 tbl olive oil
soft taco shells (optional)

Heat olive oil in skillet. Sauté mushrooms for 5 minutes (put cover on periodically to create juices). When almost done, add minced garlic. Then add seasoning at end.

SERVE WITH...
Taco Shells (soft)
Steamed kale
Guacamole (p. 4)
Cashew Cream (p. 8)
Hot Sauce (p. 7)

TERIYAKI STIR FRY
PREP 40 MIN | SERVES 4

INGREDIENTS
1 block tempeh, diced ½" cubes
4 tbl of coconut oil
3 tbl tamari
4 cups of mixed vegetables
(carrots, peas, corn, cauliflower, etc)
2 blocks of ramen rice noodles
4 cups of water
½ cup toasted sesame seeds

TERIYAKI SAUCE

INGREDIENTS
1 tbl coconut oil
3 cloves of garlic, minced
½ cup tamari
½ cup mirin
½ cup water
4 tbl honey or agave

HOW TO MAKE
First heat 2 tablespoons of coconut oil in pan and when hot, add in tempeh and brown until lightly crispy. Then douse with tamari and remove from pan.
Then add the 1 to 2 tablespoons of coconut oil to pan and quickly stir fry vegetables until tender: about 3 to 5 minutes
Boil water and follow directions to cook noodles. Strain noodles, spoon veggies and tempeh on top and pour sauce over everything. Shake sesame seeds on top and serve.

HOW TO MAKE
Heat oil in pan and sauté garlic for 1 minute. Then add tamari, mirin, water and bring to a gentle boil. Add honey or agave to taste and reduce heat. Then pour over vegetables and noodles.

SPAGHETTI SQUASH PRIMAVERA
PREP 1 HR | SERVES 4

PREPARE SQUASH FIRST
1 medium spaghetti squash, cut in half or quarters and steam or bake until done

TOMATO SAUCE
4 cups tomatoes, 1/4 in. cubes
½ medium onion, diced small
2-3 garlic cloves, minced
2 tsp basil
1 tsp oregano
1 tsp thyme
½ tsp black pepper
1 tbl olive oil

In medium saucepan, heat olive oil and lightly sauté onions and garlic for a couple of minutes, then add rest of ingredients above and simmer for 10 minutes.

THEN ADD IN THE VEGGIES
1 cup zucchini sliced
1 cup baby portobello mushrooms sliced
½ cup bell peppers

CREAMY CHEESY SAUCE (optional)
½ cup nutritional yeast flakes
½ cup water
¼ cup lemon juice
6 tbl raw tahini
2 tbl tamari
pinch of himalayan salt to taste

Mix together in small bowl. Then pour into the Tomato Sauce and heat but don't boil. Take a fork and pull out strands from the spaghetti squash. Pour sauce over noodles.

DAHL

PREP 30 MIN | SERVES 4

INGREDIENTS

2 cups red lentils (soaked for 2 hours)

1 sweet onion, diced

2 tbl spoons garlic, chopped

4 tbl spoons ginger, minced

4 tbl spoons turmeric, minced

(or 2 tsp powdered turmeric)

2 tsp mustard seeds

1 tsp salt

1 tsp black pepper

2 tbl olive oil

4 cups water

Optional (potatoes and frozen peas)

HOW TO MAKE

Heat olive oil in a pot, add onions and sauté until soft, add garlic and mustard seeds until browned, then add soaked lentils. Cover with 4 cups of boiling water and simmer about 20 minutes until lentils are cooked. Then add in ginger, turmeric, salt and pepper. Taste and see if it needs more salt or pepper. Optionally, add peas in last and don't overcook. Cook the potatoes separately (steam for 5 minutes in an Instant Pot or boil for 20 minutes over stove).

JAHAWAIIAN TEMPEH WRAPS
PREP 40 | SERVES 4

Serve with...
Mac nut or cashew cream (p. 8)
Sweet salsa & guacamole (p. 4)

TEMPEH FILLING INGREDIENTS
1 package tempeh, ½" diced cubes
½ sweet onion, chopped
4 baby portobello mushrooms, sliced
1 cup cabbage, chopped
2 tbl raw honey or agave
3 tbl coconut oil

JAHWAIIAN SPICES
Mix ¼ tsp of each: Allspice, cinnamon, ginger powder, orange & lemon zest and wasabi.

HOW TO MAKE
Heat 3 tbl coconut oil in skillet. When hot, add Tempeh and pan fry until golden brown and crispy. When done, add raw honey or agave and stir. Then add in chopped onion, mushrooms and cabbage. Stir in, and incorporate, cover with lid for a couple of minutes until done. Add salt and if necessary more sweetener to taste.

TEMPEH, LETTUCE & TOMATO SANDWICHES
PREP 40 MIN | SERVES 4

TEMPEH BACON
1 block of tempeh, sliced 1/4" thick
2 tbl of tamari
1 tsp natural liquid smoke
2 tbl olive oil

HOW TO MAKE
Heat olive oil in pan. When hot, cook tempeh until brown and crisp. Then douse with tamari and liquid smoke. Let soak in and sizzle for a minute and remove from heat.

SERVING INSTRUCTIONS
Sandwich board can include tomatoes, lettuce, red onions, sprouts, cashew or mac nut sauce and mustard.

Make your own sandwiches! Serve with sauerkraut, potatoes (page 8) and salad.

CHANA MASALA

PREP 45 MIN | SERVES 4

INGREDIENTS
1 tbl olive oil
1 small onion, finely diced
2 cloves garlic, minced
½ tsp ground cumin
½ tsp ground coriander
½ tsp turmeric
1 tsp cumin seeds
1 tsp mustard seeds
1 tsp yellow curry powder
1 tsp garam masala
¼ tsp salt
2 cups chickpeas, cooked
1 cup tomato puree
½ cup water
2 tsp fresh ginger
½ fresh green chili, minced

HOW TO MAKE
In heavy pot or cast iron skillet, heat oil to medium and add onions and garlic. Cook until soft and begin to brown, about 5 minutes. Turn heat to medium low and add spices. Stir for 1 to 2 minutes until spices become fragrant and then add tomato puree and cook for another 3 minutes. Add chickpeas and water and combine. Cover with lid and cook for 10 minutes. Lastly, add chili and ginger and incorporate, stirring for another minute. Delicious served over coconut jasmine rice or in a wrap.

SWEETS

CHAPTER 4

CINNAMON APPLE CRISP
PREP 1 HR | SERVES 6

FILLING INGREDIENTS
8 apples pealed, cored,
quartered and cut into ¼" slices
½ cup maple syrup
½ lemon juiced
1 tbl arrowroot powder
2 tsp cinnamon
⅛ tsp nutmeg
⅛ tsp allspice
dash of cloves

TOPPING INGREDIENTS
1½ cup rolled oats
¾ cup walnuts
⅓ cup gluten free flour
1 tsp cinnamon
⅛ tsp salt
2 tbl coconut oil
2 tbl maple syrup
1 tsp vanilla

HOW TO MAKE
Preheat oven to 350. In a large bowl squeeze lemon juice over sliced apples. Mix together arrowroot, cinnamon, nutmeg, allspice, cloves and then pour over the apples. Move apple mixture into a baking dish and top with the maple syrup. Cover with tin foil and bake for 35 minutes.

Prepare topping. Mix together dry ingredients (oats, walnuts, cinnamon, salt). Mix together wet ingredients (coconut oil, maple syrup, vanilla). Fold wet into dry mixing with a fork until well coated and crumbly.

When apples are done baking, remove from oven and toss. Then flatten them evenly and sprinkle the topping evenly over the apples and bake uncovered for 25 to 30 minutes until the top is crispy. Pair with cashew sweet cream if desired!

CASHEW SWEET CREAM
1 cup raw cashews or macadamia nuts (soaked 2 hours)
3 tbl maple syrup or coconut nectar
1/2 cup water
1/2 tsp vanilla extract
pinch of salt

HOW TO MAKE
Place all ingredients in a blender and blend for 1 to 2 minutes until smooth. Place in a glass container and let chill and stiffen for a couple of hours. Will stay fresh for 3 to 4 days.

BANANA BREAD
PREP 40 MIN | SERVES 4

INGREDIENTS
1 ½ cups maple syrup
1/2 cups coconut oil
3 very ripe bananas, mashed well
2 cup Red Mill gluten-free flour
½ tsp baking soda
½ cup almond milk
1 tsp apple cider vinegar
1 tsp vanilla
1 tsp cinnamon
½ tsp allspice (cloves, nutmeg)
½ tsp salt
1 cup walnuts, roughly chopped (optional)
2 tbl Bob's Red Mill Egg Replacer (mix with 4 tbl water to dissolve, let sit for one minute, then add to liquids)

HOW TO MAKE
Preheat oven to 350 F.
Grease pan with coconut oil.
Sift together flour, baking soda, salt and spices. Cream together coconut oil and maple syrup. Mix almond milk and apple cider vinegar together, then add mashed bananas and vanilla. Add the wet ingredients to the dry. Mix well. Pour batter into pan. Bake for 1 hour to an hour and 10 minutes. Prick center with knife to see if ready. It should come out clean.

SACRED CACAO BITES
PREP 30 MIN | SERVES 30

INGREDIENTS
1 tbl raw cacao butter
3 tbl coconut oil
5 tbl maple syrup or raw honey
1 pinch of Himalayan salt
1 dash of Hawaiian chili pepper (optional)
1 dash of cinnamon (optional)
1½ cup raw organic cacao powder (cold pressed)

HOW TO MAKE
Bring a pot of water to boiling. Double boil (put a bowl over the hot water so you can melt the cacao butter over indirect heat). Once the cacao butter is melted, add the maple syrup or raw local honey, salt, pepper, and cinnamon. Slowly mix in the cacao powder until it becomes a thick paste and consistency that you can form. Then roll into balls and cover the balls with cacao powder so that they don't stick to each other. Place in a Pyrex, glass or wooden container or on non toxic waxed paper. Do not store in tin foil.

ABOUT SACRED CACAO

Unlock euphoric states of awareness with sacred cacao! As raw cacao enters the bloodstream, it releases neruotransmitters, serotonin, trytophan, endorphines, dopamine, and anandanide (bliss molecule) which assist with activating those feelings we get when we fall in love. These also help with improving libido, inducing relaxation, and relieving pain and depression. Ingesting cacao can lead to deeper intimacy and the release of negative emotions blocking the heart.

Make it a sacred ritual! Before eating take a moment to ground and center. Then offer gratitude to the cacao deities and ask for any support you might be desiring in healing yourself and your relationships.

GIVE THANKS...

We love learning how to give blessings and gratitude for meals in the many languages and traditions ...

FRENCH - Bon appatite

JAPANESE - Itadakimasu

SPANISH - Buen provecho

GERMAN - Guten appetite & Lasst es euch schmecken

CHINESE - Yǒu yīgè wěidà de cān

RUSSIAN - imeyut bol'shuyu yedu

CENTRAL AMERICAN - Buen provecho

BRAZILIAN - Bom apetite! Aproveitem

CHRISTIAN - Bless this food that it can give us the strength and health we are in need.

CATHOLIC - Father of us all, This meal is a sign of Your love for us: Bless us and bless our food, And help us to give you glory each day Through Jesus Christ our Lord. Amen.

JEWISH - Barukh ata Adonai Eloheinu melekh ha'olam shehakol niyah bidvaro. Blessed are You, Lord our God, Ruler of the Universe, at whose word all came to be.

SANSKRIT - Brahmarpanam Brahma Havir Brahmagnau Brahmana Hutam Brahmaiva Tena Ghantavyam Brahmakarma Samadhina.
He alone attains Brahman who, in all actions, is fully absorbed in Brahman.
(For reference, the term 'Brahman' can be understood as source consciousness).

Thank you to our team
for your valuable input and contributions
to this recipe book!

Chef Kyra Bramble
Alyssa Hossler (content design)
Shelley Crawford (cover design)
Jacqui Gamelgaard (photography)
Andre Deslauries (video)
Suzanne Cazelais
Lindsey Depledge
Sarah Lange
Pau Suarez Gomis
Journey Jill

Thank you to our amazing Mystical Alchemy Retreat Clients who inspired us to create this book!

We love and appreciate you all!
Mahalo nui loa!
Thank you!
Ase

Heather & Donny

RECIPE REFLECTIONS

How did it go? Any substitutes or additions?
Was there anything that you would do differently?
Any great side dish ideas? How did you feel after you ate?

RECIPE :
___
___
___
___
___

RECIPE :
___
___
___
___
___

RECIPE :
___
___
___
___
___

RECIPE :
___
___
___
___
___

RECIPE REFLECTIONS

How did it go? Any substitutes or additions?
Was there anything that you would do differently?
Any great side dish ideas? How did you feel after you ate?

RECIPE :
_____
_____
_____
_____
_____

RECIPE :
_____
_____
_____
_____
_____

RECIPE :
_____
_____
_____
_____
_____

RECIPE :
_____
_____
_____
_____
_____

RECIPE REFLECTIONS

How did it go? Any substitutes or additions?
Was there anything that you would do differently?
Any great side dish ideas? How did you feel after you ate?

RECIPE :
_____
_____
_____
_____

RECIPE :
_____
_____
_____
_____

RECIPE :
_____
_____
_____
_____

RECIPE :
_____
_____
_____
_____

RECIPE REFLECTIONS

How did it go? Any substitutes or additions?
Was there anything that you would do differently?
Any great side dish ideas? How did you feel after you ate?

RECIPE :
___
___
___
___
___

RECIPE :
___
___
___
___
___

RECIPE :
___
___
___
___
___

RECIPE :
___
___
___
___
___